How One Little Word
Can Change The Way You Do Business

WORDS MATTER

Norman P. MacDonald

"After spending years looking for the key to consistently providing great customer service, Norm has given it to me in one simple word—*my*. The simplicity of *my* customers is easy to remember yet powerful enough to change a company."

A. YELEN

CONTENTS

Think Greek. 1

Set The Tone 3

Understand That Words Matter 11

Does Your Customer Service Attitude Start At The Top? 13

Look At The Big Picture First 17

Create A Want-To Environment 19

Develop Passion For The Purpose 21

How To Make A Difference 25

Be Visible And Available To Your Customers. 29

Help Your People Pay Particular Attention 31

Stay Focused On The Basics 35

How To Exceed Customer Expecations 41

Follow-Up. . . . Is It Realistic? 43

Our Customer Is Always Right—Right? 47

What Customer Service Is Not 53

Does Your Technology Help Keep Your Customers? 57

Keeping Your Customers –
How Does Your Company Measure Up? 61

Start Where It Matters Most 63

Special Thanks 67

A Word From The Author 69

THINK GREEK

"This is just the sort of nonsense up with which I will not put."
Winston Churchill

⎯⎯⎯⎯⎯⎯⎯⎯

I FIRST BEGAN TO think about the idea for this book when taking graduate courses that involved studying Greek—a language that often has nouns that are not accompanied with an article. In grammar that's called anarthrous (ă năr thrŭs). However, in English, an article such as a, the, or an will precede most nouns.

The word customer is indeed a noun and almost always takes an article. However, in the context of customer service, I believe the noun customer should never have an article. We are not in business to serve just *a* customer or *the* customer; we are in business to serve *my* customer, *your* customer, *our* customer. It's about understanding that words matter and recognizing the importance of each customer we engage and building a relationship which results in repeat business. Think of it this way:

> Customers are not *a* customer or *the* customer. They are *my* customer and *your* customer. If we fail to remember that, sooner or later, they will become someone else's customer.

SET THE TONE

"Every contact we have with a customer influences whether or not they'll come back. We have to be great every time...."

KEVIN STIRTZ

MY WIFE AND I attended a conference in Laguna Niguel, California. The conference host had us registered at the Ritz Carlton. However, they were booked solid the night before the convention started so we made arrangements to stay at the Double Tree Inn, just a mile or so down the road. The accommodations there were very nice. The staff was courteous and more than willing to assist us despite our late morning arrival - well before the official check-in time.

Though early, the Double Tree staff did not treat us as though it was an inconvenience. In fact, the associate at the front desk took care of our luggage and made every effort to get a room ready for us. This left us free to enjoy a late breakfast in the restaurant. The front desk clerk came by our table, dropped off our keys and gave us directions to our room. She indicated we could pick up our luggage when we were ready.

The next morning, before we checked out, I asked the concierge to arrange for a cab to pick us up in thirty minutes and take us to the Ritz Carlton. He said he would so we finalized our packing and took everything outside.

Thirty minutes went by, then forty-five, and still no taxi. The concierge called again (this was his third call) and the cab company said they did not have a taxi in the area and it would be another thirty minutes or more. He came over to explain the situation and said not to worry. He would take us there himself! My wife and I looked at each other with a look of doubt. But sure enough, just a few minutes later, he pulled his personal car around front and started loading our luggage in the trunk. He got on his two-way radio and told the front desk he would be back in a few minutes. Then he shuttled us to the Ritz Carlton!

Now how is that for literally going the "extra mile" in serving *your* customer!

He didn't have to do that. His boss could have said, "He can't leave the premises." They could have said it was against their company policy. There could have been numerous excuses. No one offered a single one. We did not have to rant or rave. We did not have to complain or threaten. We did not even have to ask, "Now what?" He just did the right thing by taking care of *his* customer and by solving the problem. That's customer service.

When we pulled up to the front entry at the Ritz, I asked him to stop short so that he, not the Ritz staff, could get our bags out. I tipped him generously and thanked him profusely. (If he ever reads this, BJ – thanks again my friend!)

Now to the Ritz Carlton

There may be a higher standard in hotel service than the Ritz Carlton, I am just not certain what or where it might be. The Ritz Carlton is the model for numerous books on customer service and quality.

What makes them special?

For us it started when we walked up to the entrance. The attendants out front gathered our luggage, gave us a luggage receipt and asked our name. Inside all the desk clerks were occupied with other guests, but one looked up and acknowledged us *by name!* (He knew our name because the porter had radioed it to him.) He said he would be with us shortly. When he was ready, he called us up *by name*. He already had our reservation on his computer along with our convention affiliation.

By the time we finished checking in, the bellman had our luggage and luggage receipt. He took us to our room, giving us a brief tour of the facility along the way. He also pointed out where our convention registration facilities were located and where the beach access was for that day's lunch.

Once at our room, he explained how the keys worked, how the light switch worked, where the closets were, the bathroom facilities, the reading lights, the high speed internet connections, the mini-bar, and the patio access. It was thorough, yet brief and very non-condescending.

It is important that we not lose sight of the details. Attention to details sets their service apart from the competition. Other hotels may explain how their keys work - some show you, others tell you. Some will take your luggage to the room and drop it off. Others may even take the luggage in, open the curtains and show you where the thermostat is located. But this man covered everything and did it quickly, efficiently, and in such a manner as to make us feel comfortable and at home.

That level of service continued throughout the day.

At the beach luncheon (and I do mean beach as in down by the water on the sand) there were tables with linen table cloths, linen napkins, silver service settings, a chef, four wait staff, and a full buffet with exquisite desserts. Every detail was covered for every guest.

The evening cocktail hour: heated areas for a cool evening near the beach and there appeared to be one wait staff for every 10 guests. You could serve yourself at the bar or the wait staff would get your drinks and somehow always remember who you were, where you were, and what you were drinking, even among hundreds of guests. The food was excellent. Music was at a comfortable level and tables were kept clean and uncluttered. Oh yes, did I mention white gloves on the wait staff?

Later that evening my wife and I talked about the type of service we received and other top companies that provide this caliber of customer attention. Did they do it because they were top caliber companies? Or were they top caliber companies because they provided customers with an outstanding level of service?

Had these companies grown to the point that they realized in order to keep expanding they needed to differentiate themselves and providing outstanding customer service was one way of doing that? Or, was it customer service that was driving their growth? Whichever was first, outstanding service or greatness, the Ritz Carlton understands what it takes to set them apart. That understanding allows them to charge top dollar for their service.

Now, if you have opportunity, like I did, to talk with the staff at the Ritz you'll find something very interesting. My question to several of the staff was:

"Are you as successful as you are because of the service you provide or is the service you provide a result of the success you have achieved as a company?"

To a person, their answer was the same. We are successful because of the service we provide. Several went on to explain how the extensive interviewing process and training program they received contributed a great deal to *their individual success.*

In fact, as one waitress indicated, they were "empowered" (her word, not mine) to take personal responsibility and make decisions. She continued to explain: "We are treated like adults—like ladies and gentlemen. If your beer is not cold enough, I can give you a free one. I don't have to call my manager and ask permission. I can just do it."

Treating people with respect gave everyone who worked there a sense of pride and self-esteem. In addition, it helped to reinforce their motto, "We are ladies and gentlemen serving ladies and gentlemen."

If you think that statement is non-consequential, ponder it for a while. That kind of statement conjures up an image that in itself sets a particular *mood*. It reflects a level of respect that spawns its own measure of service like water rising to its own level. There is a sense about that motto which cannot be plumbed simply by speaking it. But, when one takes it to heart and starts to flesh it out, the dynamic it creates becomes self-evident.

Combine the motto with the "Three Steps of Service" and you begin to see what distinguishes the Ritz Carlton from other hotel facilities.

THREE STEPS OF SERVICE

- A warm and sincere greeting. Use the guest's name, if and when possible

- Anticipation and compliance with guest needs

- Fond farewell. Give them a warm good-bye and use their names, if and when possible

Those with a sensitivity to customer service will notice right away that a guest's name is predominate. There is no music sweeter to the ear than the sound of one's own name. I'm a sucker for it, just like everyone else, especially when I am not quite sure how they knew it.

As Paul Harvey used to say,
"Now, the rest of the story."

One morning while at the hotel I noticed my glasses did not fit correctly. So, I decided to do a little adjusting. A tweak here and a tweak there, it wasn't long before I broke them in half. Not the kind of thing you fix with a paper clip.

"Not to worry," I thought. "I am staying at the Ritz Carlton. They can fix anything!"

I picked up my broken spectacles, walked down to the concierge's desk, laid my broken glasses on his desk and in my most pitiful voice said, "Can you help me?"

Well, it was my lucky day. I was speaking directly to the Chief Concierge.

"Sir, we do have an optometrist just down the road where we refer *our* customers. Let *me* call and see if they are open."

After a quick phone call, he indicated that the business was not open yet. He said he would be glad to call back and let me know if the optometrist could help. I explained it would probably be easier if I called and talked with them first. He then let me know he could arrange for transportation, if it was necessary.

Later that morning I called the optometrist and they were very pleasant. They indicated they would be happy to look at my lenses and see if they could match a new frame or repair my old ones.

I went back to the concierge and he arranged for a ride to the optometrist. Depending on how long the optometrist needed to fix the problem, he explained the ride would either wait for me or drop me off and come back.

Again—the *wow* factor raised its head and demonstrates that it is alive and well at the Ritz Carlton. They knew how to take care of *their* customer! In less than an hour the whole process was finished. I had new glasses and was back at the hotel!

That type of service continued until the very moment we left the facility, and I do mean the very moment we left!

Smoke and mirrors? Not at all. Genuine and sincere? Absolutely. They truly were ladies and gentlemen serving ladies and gentlemen.

Lest it get lost in my exuberance – there are two important observations:

1. Doing internal customer service right inevitably means you will be equipped to do external customer service right. For the Ritz Carlton that means, "Ladies and gentlemen serving ladies and gentlemen." They clearly reflect that concept by how they take care of their guests.

2. Never underestimate the importance of equipping your associates with the right tools to do the job. In other words, train them thoroughly to be both competent and confident. The Ritz Carlton, summarizes it like this: Anticipation and compliance with guest needs. In another portion of their "Ritz Carlton Basics" it is stated this way:

"Never lose a guest. Instant guest pacification is the responsibility of each employee. Whoever receives a complaint will own it, resolve it to the guest's satisfaction and record it."

Is your company providing the kind of service that "wows" customers? Are you doing whatever it takes to keep your customer?

UNDERSTAND THAT WORDS MATTER

*"Without knowing the force of words it
is impossible to know more."*

CONFUCIUS

———⚬⚬⚬———

WORDS MATTER. THEY matter in our everyday conversation and our writing. They also matter in our thought process. And I believe that changing words—as simple as changing articles to pronouns—matters in the way we think. Words matter in changing our perspective.

Einstein has been credited with the phrase insanity is doing the same thing over and over again and expecting different results. We could say something similar about words. When using the same words over and over we simply foster the same mindset and activity. However, if we begin using different words, we can begin to think differently and act differently.

I remember a cartoon I saw posted on a supervisor's wall. A customer stood in line at the customer service desk and the clerk behind the counter was bent over in laughter saying "You want it when!?" I suppose the cartoon was harmless in the mind of that supervisor. But it could be devastating when her associates read it knowing that mindset is apparently okay and could be replicated when dealing with customers. Was that the supervisor's expectation or intent? No. Did it send a subtle message that customers ask the impossible? You bet it did. We've all been in situations when customers expect the impossible. For some reason they think poor planning on their part constitutes an emergency on ours. Sometimes it does. That's when seeing that person as *your* customer and going the extra mile can pay huge dividends.

Ever witness this? Associates standing around – within earshot of other customers - talking about how "stupid" a customer was, or how ridiculous the person's request was, or how ignorant that person was.

I'm no saint, so I expect I have been guilty of such things. Perhaps we all have. That is not the point. The point is when we talk about customers like that we create a mindset that influences how we engage every customer. We can change that mindset by changing how we think and talk about *our* customers.

Words do matter.

Listen closely today. Listen to how the people in your company talk *about* customers. Listen to how they talk *to* customers. Listen to the words you use to talk about your customers.

DOES YOUR CUSTOMER SERVICE ATTITUDE START AT THE TOP?

"I'm not telling you it's going to be easy,
I'm telling you it's going to be worth it."

ANONYMOUS

———— ∞∞∞ ————

O UTSTANDING CUSTOMER SERVICE seldom happens unless initiated and demonstrated at the top levels of the company's leadership. If bosses do not show a commitment to serving customers how can they expect their associates to do so? If owners and managers do not provide the same level of excellent service to their associates that they do their customers how can they expect the associates to take care of customers at the highest level? If you're not convinced of this, just read the story of Nordstrom. Their whole customer service culture starts with the executives, the managers, the supervisors. As one executive notes, "It's not 'this is my department and that's your department.' It's 'this is our store, our customer, our results.'"

When working for a major office supply company I learned the value of that kind of attitude and top-down commitment to customer service. When the company made a major change in marketing strategy, our customer base seemed to double overnight. There was no way the call center staff could handle the increased volume.

To meet the demand, we hired a third party phone center in another state. Training those folks was going to be a huge challenge and a big risk. It's one thing to train people on a task, quite another to instill a culture.

We brought their training team down for a "train-the-trainer" session, which my team led, then sent them back to train their people on our system and culture. We would monitor their training via video conferencing, also something we had never done before.

One evening, while monitoring one of the training sessions, the CEO stopped by the conference room. He watched for a few minutes then turned and asked two questions:

"How are things going?"

"I think things are going fine," I replied.

Then his second question. One I was not ready for.

"Are we hurting *our* customers by doing this?"

Now what do I say? I thought hard and fast. I knew what the answer was. Using a third party call center to convey the company's culture and commitment to service was a huge risk and we all knew it. I wasn't at all sure he wanted to hear the answer to his question but he needed the truth. Gathering myself, I said straight out, "Yes, I think so—in the beginning. But in the long run I think we will be able to serve our customers better."

He paused for what seemed forever and looked away, as he was prone to do. I thought for sure he would tell me to shut it off and tell everyone to go home. But he didn't. He looked back and said, "Okay. Keep me posted on how things are going." Then he left.

Things could have ended differently. As it turned out, the move was very successful. The courage that man had to ask that question and the genuine concern he had for *his* customers was incredible. His question was not about losing money or a decrease in orders. His question was, "Are we hurting *our* customers?"

When you ask that kind of question you know you're doing customer service right! And it starts at the top.

LOOK AT THE BIG PICTURE FIRST

"Without continual growth and progress, such words as improvement, achievement, and success have no meaning."
BEN FRANKLIN

———∽∾∽———

OUTSTANDING CUSTOMER SERVICE is not just about who our customers are or what our customers need in terms of product and service. While those are important they are not central. Outstanding service results from a mindset - how we think about *our* customer and the impact our thinking has on the service we provide.

As you read some of things we talk about in this book, you may find yourself saying, "I know that," "Of course, it's so obvious," or "There's nothing profound about that." And chances are you will be right. The point is—are we practicing what we know to be true?

If we aren't putting what we know to be true into practice, what value is that knowledge? If we attend seminars and workshops, read books and learn new techniques but do not consistently implement what we learn, what value is there in gaining new information? Moreover, is all new information always appropriate?

Vince Lombardi, the legendary football coach of the Green Bay Packers, is said to have started each spring football camp with a simple illustration. According to the story, holding a football in the air, he would say, "Gentlemen, this is a football!"

His audience consisted of men who had been playing football most of their lives. They had grown up around the pigskin. Some may have known every dimple on the ball! So what was the coach's point?

IT'S ALL ABOUT THE FUNDAMENTALS.

If you listen to most interviews with coaches during any football game, pre-game or post-game, they invariably say the same thing in one form or another. "Our objective is to maintain possession of the ball, move the ball down the field, and avoid turning the ball over."

In many respects, the same fundamentals apply to customer service. The objective is to maintain a long-term relationship with our customers (possession of the ball), offer exceptional value and service (move the ball), and keep our customers by exceeding customer expectations (avoid turning the ball over).

Sounds simple, but often it's not. Most of us can attest to that based solely on the service we receive as customers. Yet, if we practice the fundamentals—do things right, do the right things, and see the buyer as *our* customer, it's a safe bet we have a winning game plan.

CREATE A WANT-TO ENVIRONMENT

*"Listen to advice and accept instruction, that
you may gain wisdom for the future."*
Prov. 19:20

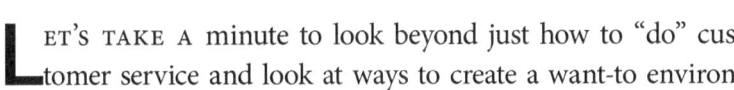

L ET'S TAKE A minute to look beyond just how to "do" customer service and look at ways to create a want-to environment where great customer service occurs naturally.

If you are an individual who serves people in any capacity, I want to invite you to think differently about how you view customers. After all, it comes down to you, the individual, interacting with customers that makes or breaks a business transaction. In many respects, you contribute to the success or failure of the business itself. Your want-to is demonstrated on the frontline with customers every single day.

If you are a Manager/Supervisor, this book is intended to give you a renewed want-to for serving *your* customers—your associates. Your associates are the very people responsible for engaging the customer first. We all get stale at times. We get so wrapped up managing things we often forget our primary responsibility is to lead people; to motivate them, to coach them, to challenge them. I am convinced that if we do not treat our associates with respect and dignity, they will never treat our customers with the respect and dignity they deserve. As a manager or supervisor, your want-to really begins with serving your associates.

If you are a business owner, I hope this book rattles you a bit. I know if you're a small business you can find yourself struggling to compete with the big boys. Nevertheless, if you offer a good product at a fair price and support that product with outstanding customer service, you can win in most any marketplace against any competition. As an owner, your want-to starts with a clear vision of success.

We need to check our glasses.

I wear glasses. If I take them off and hold them up to the light it's most likely they could stand a good cleaning. Does that prevent me from reading or seeing what I want to see? Of course it doesn't. My eyes adjust and see right through the dirt and grime.

Our company's commitment to outstanding customer service can be like that. We think we are seeing clearly but we get so accustomed to doing the same things, seeing things the same way, we're not seeing clearly. We have lost our edge. Our passion has dwindled. Our desire to keep the store neat and clean has slipped. Greeting our customers with enthusiasm has fallen off and we are no longer going the extra mile to do whatever it takes to make customers happy. We need to check our glasses.

Renewing our want-to is fundamental to keeping our vision clear. Not only that, it serves our fundamental objective; providing uncompromising customer service to our customer with every contact and transaction.

DEVELOP A PASSION FOR THE PURPOSE

"...Create a vision of perfection centered on the customer."

KEN BLACHARD AND S. BOWLES

---⸎---

SEVERAL YEARS AGO, I read this statement: "Customer Service is not a department...it's an attitude."

We have all known customer service associates with "an attitude" but that's not the intent behind the phrase. Real customer service evolves from an attitude of serving, exploring needs and solving problems.

Customers, for the most part, do not want or expect the spectacular. Too often we think they do, but they don't. When you net it all out our customer's expectations come down to this:

- They expect to be treated with respect.

- They expect to receive a good product at a fair price.

- They expect to receive a product or service that works.

- They expect to receive service after the sale, if needed.

Our responsibility is to fulfill those expectations. In a very real sense, how well we succeed at that will be the standard our customers use to define our business.

Think about the last survey you received after a store visit, or having your car serviced at the dealership, or hanging up after a call to your bank, or making an on-line purchase? Most of those surveys look at the very issues we have outlined above. Why? Those points are important—important to our customers. Yes, price plays its role, but it is not always the primary factor. If we do a good job of consistently satisfying the four points we have noted above, chances are very good we will build a strong and vibrant base of customers. Customers who will not hesitate to tell others good things about our business. Customers committed to a level of loyalty in supporting our business.

It's no secret, managing customer expectations and providing great service can result in long term loyalty.

Usually a car/truck is our most expensive investment after our house. Yet, often we look for the lowest, a.k.a. cheapest, price when it comes to having service work performed. Not me! Give me a mechanic and shop I can trust and I'll pay just about any price for them to keep my cars on the road.

We lived in Columbus, Ohio for several years. Shortly after moving there, I needed some service work on my truck. I had already experienced a couple disappointments at some local repair shops so I was not interested in repeating that. I asked around and someone recommended a local service station several miles from where we lived. Even though it was a long drive, I decided I would try them. I made an appointment and took my truck over.

When I arrived, the service manager asked all the pertinent questions, took my keys and I was off. Later that day he called with a rundown of the problem. He told me what it would cost to fix it and when the truck would be ready. The one thing I thought would be a true test was the when-it-would-be-ready part. Service shops are often notorious for not having things ready when they say. At least that is what I had come to expect. But sure enough, when I showed up at the indicated time, the truck was fixed and ready to go and at the price quoted.

From that day forward, for almost five years, those people took care of every vehicle we owned. I trusted them implicitly.

That is why I am passionate about outstanding customer service. It fosters loyalty.

A large dose of this passion I have for customer service was developed while working for a large call center. I can say, without hesitation, every meeting I was involved in focused on customer service. That was the culture of the company. Regardless of the agenda, improving customer service was the primary goal! Whether we were discussing software, hardware, dinnerware or underwear, serving our customers was the central issue—always.

Words mattered and it was all about passion for the purpose: serving our customers.

HOW TO MAKE
A DIFFERENCE

*"Words do two things; they provide food for the mind
and create light for understanding and awareness."*
JOHN ROHN

———— ∞ ————

CUSTOMERS ARE NOT neutral objects that make purchases at a business or on a website. They are individuals we form relationships with – business relationships. In some cases we want to build long-term relationships that foster loyalty and result in a positive experience both for our customers and our business.

That is why the concept of *"my* customer" is so important. When we think of customers as "a" customer or "the" customer, there is no ownership. There is no room for relationship. The interaction is neutral. But, in reality, customers expect to be treated with respect, which includes sincerity and empathy. In addition, as mentioned earlier, they expect a good product at a fair price. Furthermore they expect, if necessary, service after the sale. That is what we all want as customers. Isn't that what you want? It only comes through relationship.

Recently, I walked into the retail outlet of my cell phone provider. It's a place I have been to many times and always experienced excellent service. This time was different. Something had changed.

There were two questions I wanted to discuss with someone; a billing question and a tech question. There were six associates in the store and three customers. Nevertheless, I waited half an hour for someone to answer my billing question.

Because I have been in that store often, I had seen every one of the sales people, at one time or another, behind the billing counter. On this visit, all but two of them asked if I needed help and I replied, "I have a billing question and a tech question. The billing person is tied up and it looks like it's going to take a while." Not one person asked, "What's your question, maybe I can help?" Not one! I ultimately left over an hour later finally having both my questions answered but not feeling good about the experience.

When I seek a product or service I want to know the person I'm talking to listens to what I need or seeks to understand the problem I'm trying to solve. I want to know they care enough to ask questions, determine the real problem, or need, and offer the correct solution or product the first time. Get me taken care of the first time so I don't need to come back.

Once I was involved in an on-line chat session with a so-called parts specialist from a major department store. I had gone online to look at parts for our washing machine and the chat window popped up so I figured what the heck.

I typed in a description of what I was looking for and he said it was part so-and-so and sent a link with a diagram. As I scrolled through the diagram, I hesitated and typed back, "Wait, I *think* the part I need is this…" He replied, "Okay, would you like me to ship that out today. I'm certain that's the correct part."

"Really?" I mumbled to myself, "A minute ago you were certain the other part was what I needed."

I replied, "You may be certain but I'm not". He proceeded to push for the sale knowing full well neither of us knew for sure what part was needed. It became obvious to me, I was not on the road to receiving the correct solution to my problem. I was on the road to disappointment and frustration.

When we think of customers in neutral or impersonal ways, it is easy to avoid providing them with excellent customer service and not feel bad about it. It's easy to simply say I'm certain that's the correct part and not really engage customers with fact-finding questions. However, when we see customers as *our* customers then we serve them in a manner that can result in both parties feeling confident about the sale. As one Nordstrom executive so aptly put it,

> "*Customers want to do business with those retailers who understand their needs and desires...*"

That kind of attitude is what makes a difference and sets your business apart from all others.

BE VISIBLE AND AVAILABLE TO YOUR CUSTOMERS

"Be everywhere, do everything and never fail to astonish the customer.

Macy's Motto

When browsing the web I ran across a story about a lake in Chile that completely disappeared. According to local park rangers, one day it was there and the next time they went by it was gone. There was nothing there but a few chunks of ice bearing evidence of what once was. We're not talking about a pond, we're talking about a lake that was 10-12 acres in size—gone! Amazing!

What's gone but not so amazing? Try going into a big box store and looking for some personal assistance. It's all too often analogous to that lake. All the associates are gone! One minute, when you don't need them, they seem to be everywhere. The next minute, when you do need them, they're gone. It's like some giant fissure opened up and swallowed them!

Now I will admit, some of these big box stores are getting better. In the past, you would walk into the store and there would be employees all over the place blocking the aisle, putting up inventory and sometimes just milling around. Some have changed their method of operation. Apparently they realized it is not enough to have products available for price conscious shoppers and the do-it-yourselfer. They need to serve their customers and provide assistance if they want to gain a bigger market share.

Be Visible and Available

Whether it's a company with two employees or two hundred, we cannot stress enough that customers must feel welcome and know help is available when they need it. Creating that kind of environment is harder to do than you might think. Some associates don't want to be bothered or have their workflow interrupted. That can be management's fault for stressing the wrong priorities. Then too, there are those employees who often try to avoid customers.

One retail store I worked for went through a period where we were to contact customers, what seemed like, every thirty seconds. It got to the point where customers, on more than one occasion, would tell us to leave them alone. That's hovering and hovering is annoying to customers. There is a huge difference between hovering and being available.

Over the years, at a local do-it-yourself big box store, I have noticed varying levels of service. Recently, I stopped by to pick up a few items for the yard and as I walked to the particular department a young man made eye contact and greeted me. A few minutes later he came back and asked if I had any questions or needed any help. He didn't hover and he definitely did not ignore me. He did what he needed to do in order to take care of his customer. He was visible and available. That is exactly how most customers want it.

HELP YOUR PEOPLE PAY PARTICULAR ATTENTION

"Customers are not a customer or the customer. They are my customer and your customer. If we fail to remember that, sooner or later they will become someone else's customer."

AUTHOR

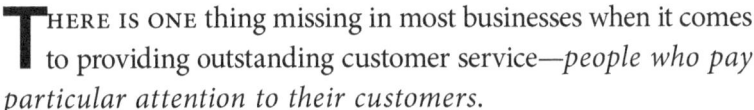

THERE IS ONE thing missing in most businesses when it comes to providing outstanding customer service—*people who pay particular attention to their customers.*

We have all seen the television ads with model-like, friendly and knowledgeable associates there to answer your questions and help you at every turn. They flash the Cheshire smile as their company boasts of service muscle.

I would like to know where those people work. I seldom receive the kind of service touted in those ads. Usually I'm lucky to get any assistance at all unless I go looking for someone. Am I alone in this?

One holiday season my wife and I visited a local department store. As we walked in the door, it seemed they had just hired a platoon of workers for the upcoming holiday season.

It appeared some training was going on and that was a good thing. Since the store was not busy there was a good opportunity for supervisors to offer some coaching.

While we were shopping, the group dismissed and here's what we observed. Two or three associates standing around talking, another one on her cell phone, two more gathered around a supervisor or manager and a few were aimlessly walking around fondling merchandise. Not once did anyone offer us assistance nor did they speak to any other customer as far as we could tell. No one seemed to be paying particular attention to customers in the store. Now there is definitely something wrong with that picture.

Let's compare that to another experience in a major office supply store. There were red shirts everywhere. We must have been approached by two or three different associates within the first several minutes. They definitely were paying particular attention to their customers.

When I asked one associate about a specific item, she took me directly to it. When I asked a question about the item, she did not know the answer. Instead of making something up or stopping with "I don't know," she said what every friendly, knowledgeable associate should say – "Sir, I don't know the answer to that question, but let me find out for you." Little doubt that I was *her* customer and she was going to take care of me.

Are we getting the picture? It is not hard. But it does take a change in mindset for some people.

As with the Coach Lombardi story, it goes back to fundamentals like:

- Greet the customer

- Offer assistance at the first opportunity

- Meet the customer's needs efficiently

- Say "Thank You" at the end

To emphasize those fundamentals, here is another story that begins with grocery stores and ends with an office supply store (yep, we spend a lot of time in office supply stores).

When we first moved to North Carolina we needed to eat so we started shopping for groceries. We sampled two or three different stores looking for one where we could buy the majority of our groceries. We wanted a clean, friendly store and one close to home.

As you know, just about every store has a magic card that gets you extra savings and tracks your purchases. The cards for the local stores were completely different from the stores where we shopped in Texas. Of course, as we were checking out at these different stores, a cashier would ask if we had one of their cards. We would simply say, "No. We just moved here from Texas."

Not one time—that's right, not one time out of three occasions in one store, two in another, and one in a third, did the checkout person ask us if we would like to get one of their cards. No one seemed to be paying particular attention to what we were saying. It was obvious, we were just *a* customer to them and they really did not care if we shopped there or not. Let's remember, perception is reality for most people and we got the message loud and clear.

Okay, let's look at a much different side of the rewards card concept.

We stopped at a local big box office supply store to pick up a few things. To our pleasure, we were greeted as we entered the store and had some terrific service while shopping. As we were checking out, the young woman asked us if we had a rewards card. As before, we replied "No. We've just moved here from Texas."

Guess what she said next? (I'm thinking she was taught the value of paying particular attention to her customer.)

"Would you like to receive one? It only takes a few minutes and you can save on today's purchase and all future purchases."

"Well of course we would," my wife replied and the cashier began gathering the necessary information.

What a dramatic difference that was from our previous experiences at the grocery stores.

That office supply store had earned a customer!

That is what customer service is all about. That's what it means to pay particular attention to your customers.

I don't know the author, but a quote I've heard often over the years reflects what we've just been writing about:

> *More businesses close because of the attitude of indifference on the part of employees than from lack of capital.*

STAY FOCUSED ON THE BASICS

"To add real service you must add something which cannot be bought or measured with money, and that is sincerity and integrity."

DONALD A. ADAMS

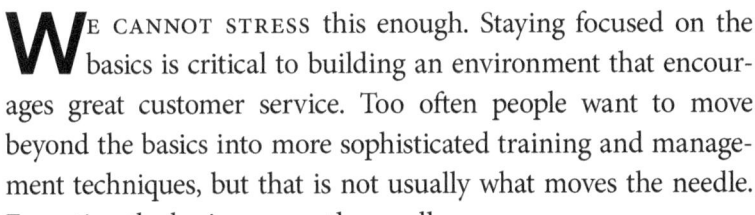

WE CANNOT STRESS this enough. Staying focused on the basics is critical to building an environment that encourages great customer service. Too often people want to move beyond the basics into more sophisticated training and management techniques, but that is not usually what moves the needle. Executing the basics moves the needle.

Some of the basics we have talked about already:

- Treat your customers with respect.

- Provide your customers with a good product at a fair price.

- Provide your customers with a product that works.

- Provide your customers with service after the sale, if needed.

Now we will look at some others.

Approach your customer with the intent of establishing a long-term relationship.

For business to thrive we need repeat business. As the saying goes, it takes months to find a customer...seconds to lose one. We want to keep customers. We want customers coming back. We want customers telling their friends and neighbors about us. Providing our customers with the best product and/or service each time they interact with our business is essential to establishing that long-term relationship. It's not easy and takes a concerted effort every time we interact with our customer. We cannot let our guard down for a second. Nor can our associates.

Avoid letting policy get in the way of people.

The last thing customers want to hear is, "It's our policy that..." or "It's against our policy to..." Realistically, the only policy any business should have is to take care of their customer. We will seldom lose customers because we went against policy. We will most surely lose customers if we let policy get in the way of solving our customer's problem or meeting their need.

Communicate, communicate, communicate...

Everyone who has anything to do with customers, needs to know what's happening within the business. That does not mean knowing every financial metric or what color we plan to paint the walls. However, associates do need to know critical information that enables them to serve their customers.

If we take on a new product, let everyone know what that product is and where it is located. When it's appropriate, teach them to use the product and explain how customers can benefit from the product.

If we change a store layout, add a new planogram, or change a telephone script, we need to let everyone know what has changed and where they can find things. It may seem like no big deal to us, but it ensures our associates are informed and lets them know we are keeping them up-to-date.

Have key phone numbers or extensions available for everyone. At one place I worked, I can't tell you how many times someone would come on the two-way radio and ask, "What's the number for such and such department?" or "What's our fax number?" A simple laminated information sheet at each phone can provide the needed information seamlessly.

> Pay particular attention to the
> customer right in front of you!

This is an issue many, especially retail businesses, neglect. More often than we should, we see associates treating customers on the phone as a priority while ignoring customers standing at the counter.

I know phone calls come to businesses non-stop during the day. But it's frustrating, as a customer, to have someone complete a transaction on the phone while keeping me, their in-person customer, waiting to complete my purchase.

There is nothing wrong with saying to the customer on the phone, "Sir, I'm with another one of *my* customers. May I put you on hold while I finish taking care of them, or would you prefer we call you back?"

Here is what happened to me when calling a local bookstore. When I asked the woman if they had a certain book in stock she replied, "May I put you on hold while I finish with *my* customer then I will be happy to check and see if we have the book in stock. Is that okay?"

Really, she really said that. Of course it was okay. After all, I was next in line to be *her* customer!

Be vigilant with the obvious.

These are things we know we should do, but often don't:

- Use our customer's name when appropriate.

- Get out from behind the counter so we can engage our customer.

- Pay attention to what our customer is saying beyond their words: tone of voice, body language, rate of speech.

- Be polite and courteous even when it's hard.

In addition, keep in mind, when customers get frustrated or angry, we may be the NRP: Nearest Responsible Person. Because we are the NRP, they vent at us. It is important not to take things personally. Let them vent. Pay particular attention to everything they say. Let them get it all out, every bit of it. Let them talk until they are done. Then ask, "Is there anything else?" Once they are done, exercise due diligence to solve the problem or meet the need.

Serving customers is not a selling game.

Let's help our customers buy what will solve their problem or meet their need.

In other words, we need to be certain we understand what the product or service is *our* customer is looking for. Ask questions to gain a clear understanding. We should not assume we know what they are looking for or even that they know what they are looking for.

When my wife and I first moved into our home I realized the house did not have a digital thermostat. Having brought the thermostat from our previous home, I downloaded the instructions for it and quickly made the installation.

One morning, when the outside temperature had dropped dramatically and the heat was supposed to be on, there was nothing but cold air blowing from the registers. I checked everything. According to the instructions the thermostat was installed correctly. Even though it was set on "heat", only cold air was coming out. I checked the unit outside and everything seemed fine.

Since we had purchased a home warranty I contacted the warranty company. They said they would have an HVAC company contact us to arrange a service call. A company called within the hour and came to our home that morning. (Did you get that last sentence?)

When the service company arrived they asked if the thermostat was programmed correctly. I explained how I had only switched out the old unit with the digital one based on the instructions. Then the service technician, who was also the owner of the company, asked,

"Do you have a heat pump?"

"Yes," I replied.

"Are you sure it's a heat pump?" he pressed.

"I think so. It's outside and it's all one unit. What else could it be?"

"Where's it located?"

I told him and he went to look.

A few minutes later he came back and with a smile and said, "It's not a heat pump. It is a combined heating and cooling system. If you have the thermostat programmed for a heat pump that explains why it's blowing cold air."

I felt a bit embarrassed. He didn't make me feel that way. My own ignorance made me feel that way. He was nice about it and in a few minutes had everything fixed and hot air flowing.

The reality is, I had no idea what that thing was on the side of my house. We have always had furnaces on the inside and AC units on the outside. Nevertheless, through patient probing and a kind demeanor, he determined the problem and fixed it.

You can imagine how easy it would have been for him to take me down the river with some fictitious service work or, at the least, sell me a new expensive thermostat. He did neither of those things. Why? I was *his* customer!

Did I call him again? Absolutely I did. Did I recommend him? Absolutely I did.

As a customer, don't sell to me. Help me buy the product or service that will solve my problem or meet my need and never sell me something I do not need or do not want. It violates the trust factor.

Keep these basics in mind and you will go a long way in keeping your customers.

HOW TO EXCEED CUSTOMER EXPECTATIONS

"The first step in exceeding your customer's expectations is to know those expectations.

ROY H. WILLIAMS

COMMON SENSE SAYS exceeding our customer's expectations with every transaction or engagement is challenging. That does not mean we don't try.

Whenever we can exceed our customer's expectations—let's do it.

Whenever our associates can exceed their customer's expectations—let them do it.

What I have realized over the past twenty some years, it does not take a great deal to wow our customer.

My wife and I decided to take a last minute overnight trip one 4th of July. The ultimate decision was take the dog or leave the dog. Taking the dog meant driving the truck and not the motorcycle. Boarding the dog meant taking the motorcycle and having a ton more fun.

Knowing our options for boarding the dog were limited on

such short notice, I stopped by our veterinarian's office. It was the day before we intended to leave so I tried to manage my expectations. The young woman checked the reservations list and they were booked solid. Then her eyes got wide as saucers.

"When will you be picking up your pet?" she asked.

"On Friday."

"Great," she said. "We can put your dog in the grooming area since the groomer will also be gone on vacation those days."

Talk about exceeding customer expectations. I was elated that she did not stop thinking after checking the book. She went one step further and was able to meet *her* customer's need. Our need!

It is often the simple gestures that "wow" our customers. We don't always need to go the extra mile. It does not take the extreme to be the cream.

The story is often told about Nordstrom's department store taking back car tires when they didn't even sell car tires. As Robert Spector and Patrick McCarthy tell in their book *The Nordstrom Way to Customer Service Excellence*, the story goes like this:

"In 1975, Nordstrom acquired three stores in Alaska from the Northern Commercial Company, a full-line department store that sold many products, including tires. After Nordstrom bought the stores, the company…eliminated lots of departments, including the tire department. So, when a customer – who purchased the tires in that building from Northern Commercial (not Nordstrom) – brought them back to Nordstrom, the return was accepted."

That story is definitely over-the-top but it's not what most of us encounter on a daily basis. If you want to know how to exceed customer expectations, understand that words matter. Begin thinking and acting like "Hey, this is *my* customer. What can I do to make sure I take care of them?" Then go about the business of doing it.

FOLLOW-UP...
IS IT REALISTIC?

"The key to organized, diligent follow-up is prioritizing."

ADRIENNE ZOBLE

THERE HAVE BEEN occasions when we have hired someone to mow our yard. On one such occasion, I hired a man who was just starting his lawn mowing business. He did a nice job. When he finished I thanked him and paid him. Before leaving he gave me a few business cards and asked if I would refer him when the opportunity came up. Something I was happy to do, but not right away. I waited a couple of weeks to see if he would call me back. He never did.

He was starting a new business, had at least one satisfied customer who was willing to recommend him, and never once followed up. Why?

Following up with our customers or potential customers is not always realistic. But more often than not it's easier than we think. If someone visits our store and fills out information that we have requested, follow up. If they have visited our web page and filled out a "contact" form, follow up. If they have called and left a message for a return call, follow up. And always follow up in a timely manner.

We recently purchased a new rocker recliner. My wife had been after me for years to replace my old worn out chair so when we found a good recliner at a fair price we jumped on it.

After a few days, my wife noticed the chair was making noises when I rocked and we both noticed a creaking sound when I rocked a bit more aggressively. Since the chair was under warranty, I decided to contact the store. It was a Saturday when I went to their website and filled out the contact form stating my concerns. My wife chuckled and said it was unlikely I would hear back.

Within a few hours, they sent an email back asking at which store the chair was purchased. I replied. They sent a second email saying the chair was under warranty and they would contact the person who does their repairs. On Sunday, they sent a third email with the person's name and indicating he would call to make arrangements to come to the house and look at the chair. Then again, on Sunday, they sent a fourth email saying if I had not heard from that person before the end of the week to call them.

Really, they did all that – on the weekend!

The technician called on Monday and showed up that afternoon to take care of the problem.

I once had a customer looking for a typewriter ribbon they were having trouble finding. I did a few quick searches for them in our catalog and on-line and could find nothing. She was frustrated that no one seemed to carry the ribbon that she needed despite the fact it was an old typewriter and the ribbon she held in her hand had seen better days. I apologized that I could not find anything but told her I would do some more searching. If she would leave me her phone number, I would let her know what I found out.

That afternoon, after I got home, I did some searching on the internet and finally found the brand of ribbon she needed and at least one store that had one, and only one, in stock. I gave her a call and provided the information. As we talked, she was more pleased that I had called her back, as I told her I would, than she was about finding a place to buy her typewriter ribbon. Not a big deal in the scheme of things, but a wow factor for her.

Getting back to our customers is one important way to develop a positive relationship with them. Advertisers call it "top-of-mind awareness". When customers think of a product or service appropriate to our business we want them to think of us! A simple phone call, post card, letter, or email tells customers we appreciate the opportunity to serve them.

Make follow-up a routine business practice. It sets you apart from the competition and paves the way to keeping your customers.

OUR CUSTOMER IS ALWAYS RIGHT – RIGHT?

"The value of pleasing a customer is more important than the cost."

Armen Kabodia

———— ❧ ————

I S OUR CUSTOMER always right? Let's answer that with another question.

When is our customer wrong?

Quite simply, our customer is always right even if it is only in his or her own mind. Frequently, somehow or someway, they have been wronged and they want things corrected or they believe they know what they need and they cannot be convinced otherwise.

Arguing with our customer about the rightness or wrongness of a circumstance is seldom productive. It is the old push-and-push-back syndrome. When customers push with their feelings and a store representative decides to push back, something is going to give. It is imperative to make sure that does not happen. How?

After we have let them vent and get everything out so we have a clear understanding of what the problem is, say something like this:

"I apologize that you had that experience. I understand why you *feel* that way. I would have *felt* the same way in similar circumstances. What I've *found* is this..." Then offer them a solution or resolution that could bring the situation to a satisfactory close. Apologizing and using *feel, felt, found* can help customers gain new information. Often, new information leads to a new decision.

Whether owner, manager, supervisor, or associate – it is our job to apologize when there's a problem. It does not mean the situation was personally our fault. However, it was our company that made the "mistake" or created the confusion and our customer is experiencing the consequences. Apologize for the problem, for the rude behavior of an associate, for the damage to a product, for unacceptable service, for incorrect pricing, for whatever. Apologize and then fix it.

Does apologizing and using something like "feel, felt, found" always work? No. Is there a time when our customer needs a little shove? Perhaps, but that is not the point. Our primary objective is to *serve* our customer not *sever* our relationship.

I called a local shop to take my truck in for an oil change, tire balance, and rotation. The person I spoke with said they were busy, it may take an hour or so, but they could work it in.

I showed up not ten minutes after I called. He said it would be at least an hour and a half. Okay, no big deal, I'll do some shopping at the mall. After almost two hours passed, my truck was still sitting in the lot where I parked it. I was not happy.

I asked about it and the technician said, "I'm not sure when we'll get to it. We're a bit backed up."

I reminded him of his time commitment both when I called

and when I came in. It fell on deaf ears. So I said, "Give me my keys. I'm leaving."

On my way out the door, he hollers at me, "We'll get to it as quick as we can. We're really busy."

"You should have told me that on the phone or when I came in. I could have come back. As it is, I'll just take it somewhere else."

"Oh, you won't get in anywhere else any faster," he said.

"Don't count on it!"

"I've been in the automotive business for 14 years," he continued. "I know what I'm talking about."

I quickly did an about-face, marched back, and looked him square in the eyes, "Do you know who I am? I'm your customer! You don't ever argue with your customer!" And out the door I went.

If we step back, let's look at how this might have gone when I asked for my keys.

He could have said, "I apologize for the delay. Obviously this is taking longer than I anticipated. I know how frustrated you must *feel*. I've *felt* the same way in similar circumstances. Can I put you down for first thing tomorrow morning? For the inconvenience, we'd be happy to rotate the tires at no charge."

Would I have accepted his offer? I don't know. What I do know is the situation would have ended better than it did. As it is, I have not been back in one of those shops in years.

That brings me to the importance of giving our associates both the responsibility and authority to do what it takes to make customers happy. If a situation escalates and management is going to take care of the customer anyway, why let the situation escalate? Let your associate take care of it immediately. In most instances, you will not be disappointed.

Anytime we have to hesitate with our customers or postpone

making a decision, it opens the door of doubt in their mind. It adds to their frustration and it gives them cause for concern. Too often customers think we don't care or they are going to have to keep arguing up the line until they get satisfaction. Why not nip it at the start? Let our associates do what needs to be done right then and there to take care of *their* customer – to take care of *your* customer.

In an old movie called *Heat*, starring Al Pacino and Robert DeNiro, Pacino plays a detective intent on pursuing and capturing the bad guy (DeNiro). DeNiro plays the mastermind criminal determined on eluding the law and making the big score.

There is one scene where the two adversaries meet over a cup of coffee. After a long conversation they both acknowledge, even though they have now met face to face, neither would hesitate to kill the other. As DeNiro puts it, "I would not hesitate, not for a second."

In the final scene, the two are chasing each other through an airport runway area. As Pacino comes into an open field, a plane overhead lit up the area around him. DeNiro steps from behind his cover to take the fatal shot, but hesitates. Pacino sees a shadow, turns and fires four shots into DeNiro.

One did indeed hesitate. That hesitation cost him his life.

IN BUSINESS, HESITATION COULD COST US OUR CUSTOMER.

Avoid phrases like:

- "I'll have to check with my supervisor."
- "Let me talk to my manager."
- "We'll get back to you."

All of those open the door for doubt, concern, and frustration. It is not a matter of whether the customer is right or wrong. Shut the door of doubt as soon as possible.

As fans of great customer service, let's learn from one of the critical components of Nordstrom's success. They move decision making to the front line. In fact, Rule #1 in their Code of Service is

"Use your good judgment in all situations".

WHAT CUSTOMER SERVICE IS NOT

"Make a customer not a sale."

KATHRINE BARCHETTI

———∞∞∞———

CUSTOMER SERVICE IS not selling. Selling is selling. Customer service is serving.

Before I alienate some of you, let me hasten to add I have a great deal of respect for professional sales people. We've been there and done that. So this is not an indictment of the business of selling products or services that people need and want. However....

As a national brand mattress company says in their ad, "When you walk into a traditional mattress store *it's really not about you...*"

Much too often, a selling environment is all about getting as much product in the hands of the customer as possible and expanding the infamous average transaction. It seldom is about "you" and has little, if anything, to do with helping customers solve a problem or meet a need.

On the other hand, if we treat *our* customers with respect, pay particular attention to their needs, and see legitimate opportunities for them to get the products or services they need, then we're talking about great customer service. We may call it selling, but engaging our customer, asking questions, and taking a personal interest goes way beyond the normal idea of selling. It becomes relational. It's about building a relationship so we understand our customers and offer them exactly what they need and want, not what we think they should buy.

When purchasing my first flat screen television, from my perspective, it was going to be a straightforward transaction. I would walk into the store, find the one I wanted, make the purchase, take it home, plug it in and live happily ever after! Not even close.

Thankfully, the person I talked with saw me as *his* customer. He asked plenty of questions and then gently, but confidently, walked me through the issues involved when buying my first flat screen television. I was so thankful. If I had not been *his* customer, I would have made a huge mistake, gone home and watched nothing except my frustration level rise. Sure, he could have sold me what I thought I wanted and snickered to his buddies "He'll be back, just watch," as I walked out the door. That's not what happened. Instead, because of building a relationship, asking good questions and listening intently, he helped me buy the television that matched my needs and I instantly became a loyal customer.

Ultimately, great customer service results in long-term, on-going sales. As noted earlier, it's all about relationships. Recently I experienced that type of "selling" when trying to purchase some new stain for our deck. When I asked the salesperson for a matching color they were unable to read the color code on the old can and offered some possible matches. I was fine with anything close since we were just putting lipstick on a pig. But this person went the extra mile. He asked one of his associates to go in the back and match the color in the can I brought. Thirty minutes later he came out with what I considered a perfect match. And it was.

After finishing the deck my wife was talking about painting one of the bedrooms. I politely told her, "That's fine, but we're buying the paint from those folks." That's what meeting a customer's need will win you almost every time. A loyal customer and repeat sales.

Is your business interested more in the transaction or your customer's need? Is it more about building the bottom line or building relationships in order to keep your customers?

DOES YOUR TECHNOLOGY HELP KEEP YOUR CUSTOMERS?

"If you make customers unhappy in the physical world, they might each tell 6 friends. If you make customers unhappy on the Internet, they can each tell 6,000 friends."

JEFF BEZO, AMAZON

TELEPHONY AND TECHNOLOGY make our world flatter and at times better. However, telephone Voice Response Units (VRUs) and technology can also get out of control. It is almost like we've given technology the reins of our business. Somewhat overstated I know, but not by much.

We called our cell phone provider about a specific email issue my wife was having with her phone. The technician remotely took over her phone to see if they could resolve the problem. We were impressed. Not only impressed but the problem was solved quickly and efficiently.

When you consider the impact of technology, whether it's regarding your phone, your satellite or cable provider, or a local retailer's credit card department, there's very little that cannot be done through voice response units or technology. But...

That type of technology and "efficiency" has the potential to alienate customers. Here are some ways that can happen:

- Customers get stuck in loops preventing them from getting to a real person

- Often customers are forced on hold and then fed this message, "We appreciate your patience. Your business is important to us. We will be with you momentarily." Really? If customers are really important, let's staff sufficiently to answer their call. Yes, I know every business gets over-whelmed at times whether due to weather, ill-ness or technical breakdowns. I also know that businesses call centers must push the edge of the envelope when it comes to staffing based on call volumes. I understand all that. However, if we put off our customers as a general business practice just because we don't want to make the extra investment—it seems to me there's some-thing amiss in that idea.

When it comes to actually having a live person answering the business phone, all too often we forget that our customer may be calling for the first time. Our associate answering the phone has done so for the umpteenth time. The asso-ciate knows the business name, their name, and the company slogan or sales pitch. However, our customer may be hearing it for the first time. Encourage everyone who answers the busi-ness phone to slow down! Let's give customers the opportu-nity to hear and understand what's being said.

Today, yesterday, or certainly within the last week you have most likely visited a company's website. Did you find the site difficult to navigate? Did you look at tab after tab before finding the information you wanted? Did you find information that was out of date?

There is nothing magical when it comes to internet marketing and social media. It can be effective and efficient. However, with today's internet-savvy consumers, it is imperative that our on-line presence be maintained properly and be up-to-date. I recall checking a locksmith's website and he offered a coupon that had expired two years prior!

Just one more thing. Do you have a list of contact numbers and email addresses on your website? If you do, please respond to people when they reach out to you. Not a month or so down the road, but try your best to get back within twenty-four hours. It will go a long way toward building customer loyalty and keeping your customer. With little hesitation, I can say almost 75% of the time, when I've contacted a company's customer service staff or an individual listed on the website, I have not gotten a response. If I did, it was often days, if not weeks, after the initial contact. Even as I type this, I have been waiting several months for a response to an inquiry I made through a website.

One quick, positive story about this topic. My wife and I were looking to do some modifications to our back deck. It was a Saturday afternoon when I did a quick internet look-up on a company we had used years ago in a different state. Once I located their local website, I filled out the contact information and hit "send." Literally, within forty-five minutes my phone rang. It was the *owner* of the company following up on my inquiry and wanting to set a time to come out and look at our project!

If you own your own business or are the CEO of a business, do yourself a favor, stay involved in your business operations.

Call your business and listen to how your associates answer the phone. Regularly check your web presence. Find out if your company's information is correct and up to date. See if the website is easy to navigate. Pretend to be your customer and see how painless, or painful, it is to place an order or get information. Don't always rely on someone else to manage your company's presence. Let's be real; you would never tolerate a newspaper printing your ad incorrectly, a radio station giving the wrong address, or a mass mailer sending an outdated coupon. It is your company's image at stake. Take an active role in making sure it is correct.

Words matter. Be certain your technology is not interfering with serving and keeping your customers.

KEEPING YOUR CUSTOMERS - HOW DOES YOUR COMPANY MEASURE UP?

"We must remember that people will continue to do business with those who give good service, and certainly there is never a traffic jam on that extra mile. Performance will continue to outsell promises. Enthusiasm will be as contagious as ever. Know-how will surpass guess-how. And trust, not tricks, will keep your customers loyal."

MARY KAY

—⌘—

I SUSPECT, IF WE think back on the basic or fundamental steps we know to take but often don't, we will certainly uncover potential areas of improvement that will help us keep our customers.

Check the bookshelves at any brick and mortar bookstore or on-line. When it comes to the category of customer service, there are titles like "The Keys to ..., the Magic of ..., The Secret to ...," etc. What is it about the human thought process that propels us to look for a magic bullet or panacea? Whether it's business, personal success, relationships or making friends, it seems we're always looking for an easy solution. Building relationships in order to keep your customers takes work. There is nothing magical about it.

My wife and I have been married over thirty years. It has not just happened that way. Nor is that longevity a result of ignoring one another, failing to help one another, or not wanting to be with one another. It came from hard work. We work on our relationship every day. We cultivate trust. We strive to serve one another whether helping with chores or supporting one another in our careers. I would rather be with her than anyone else. Every bit of what I have just described didn't just happen. It has taken initiative on both our parts for over thirty years. In addition, I might add, we are looking forward to another thirty years.

The same is true when providing uncompromising customer service. We cannot expect good things and right thinking to just happen. We must do the basics, do them well, and do them daily. We must encourage the same in others. Great customer service takes commitment and time. We may never get everyone in our company on board one hundred percent, but that should not stop us from cultivating a culture that says we take care of the customer no matter what.

START WHERE IT MATTERS MOST

*"If you're not serving the customer, your job
is to be serving someone who is."*

JAN CARLZON

WE OBSERVED EARLIER that the culture that perpetuates outstanding customer service originates at the top. It is how owners treat managers, how managers treat supervisors, how supervisors treat associates, and how associates treat customers.

If we are not doing internal customer service well, then whatever we do to promote or teach external customer service will ultimately fail. Ken Blanchard, Jim Ballard, and Fred Finch, in their book *Customer Mania,* make this point:

> *"Common sense says that if you consistently treat those who serve customers as if they're the most important people in the company, they will treat customers as if they're the most important people in the world."*

Ray Johnson, former co-chairman of Nordstrom says it this way:

> *"The only thing we have going for us is the way we take care of our customers and the people who take care of our customers are on the floor".*

Christopher Hummer, President for Carolinas Medical Center –Pineville, NC echoes the same sentiment with this observation: –

> *"Our leadership team is committed to sustaining a culture where our teammates feel respected and valued, take pride in their work and their relationships, and are driven by our mission and core values."*

The bottom line is indeed the bottom line. Words matter. When we treat associates with respect and dignity they will treat customers with respect and dignity. That is the way to keep our customers.

WORDS MATTER

SPECIAL THANKS

Many good people have contributed to the thoughts expressed in this book. To name them all is not practical. However, I will say a special thanks to my "red pen" specialist, the love of my life, Alice MacDonald. She's my best friend and greatest fan. Brain T. Cox who patiently endured my good intentions. I am also grateful to Jerry Jenkins for not only reading the book but offering productive suggestions which spawned a totally new version from the original book "Customers R Anarthrous". And, of course, my thanks to Joy Gage for her consultation on the text. She has mentored me in other areas of writing and I was pleased she took on this project.

A WORD FROM THE AUTHOR

IF YOU WERE to read my lifetime resume, you would find a work history including everything from pumping gas and hauling bricks to building storage sheds. You would find business consulting, delivering propane, leading congregations, directing music, and training call center associates. Every one of those jobs, and many others, involved serving *my* customers in one form or another.

With over forty years of experience both doing customer service and teaching it, I have concluded that many companies overlook key elements when it comes to offering excellent service to their customers. These elements involve more than customers at the register, at the other end of the phone, or on a website. They also involve internal customers – our associates.

I would welcome your comments and feedback on this book. You can visit my website or contact me by email.

http://normmacdonald2.com

normmacdonald2@gmail.com

WORDS MATTER

Customers are not *a* customer or *the* customer. They are *my* customer and *your* customer. If we fail to remember that, sooner or later, they will become someone else's customer.